Troutwatching

poems by

Dallas Crow

Finishing Line Press
Georgetown, Kentucky

Troutwatching

ACKNOWLEDGMENTS

Some of these poems have previously appeared in the following publications:

Blue Earth Review
Cloudbank
Concho River Review
Connecticut River Review
Cottonwood
Florida Review
Flyfish Journal
Free State Review
Lake Effect
Louisiana Literature
Pembroke Magazine
Poet Lore
RHINO
Salamander
San Pedro River Review
Talking River Review
Tar River Poetry
Thin Air

Publisher: Leah Huete de Maines
Editor: Christen Kincaid
Cover Art and Design: Wyatt Crow
Author Photo: Dallas Crow

Order online: www.finishinglinepress.com
also available on amazon.com

Author inquiries and mail orders:
Finishing Line Press
PO Box 1626
Georgetown, Kentucky 40324
USA

Contents

For Jo 1

Consolation on the Susitna 2

Playing Ping-Pong with My Son 3

Continuity Is for the Birds 4

Dogless 5

On Pumpkins 6

Pizza and Poetry: A Manifesto 7

Songs in a Narrow Time 9

Ground Truthing in Hastings, Minnesota 13

North Coast 14

A Gathering of Stones 15

My Nature Poem 16

The Prose Poem and Common Household Appliances 17

The Prose Poem and the Art Museum 18

Notes on the Prose Poem 19

Notes Found on a Napkin in a Diner Outside Dayton, Ohio 20

The Years 21

Current Events 22

Patriotic 24

Saturday Night, Port Townsend 25

Another Mystery Train 26

Letter to Fitz from Big Sky 27

Self Portrait in a Hollywood Western 29

Portrait of my Friend Betty as a Deer Foraging in Her Own
    Back Yard 30

Bus Stop, Lagos 31

"The Barn" by John Wilde 32

Today's Image of a Black Hole 33

The Age of Miracles 34

Troutwatching 35

Appalachian Thanksgiving 36

For Jo

There's a divot in my heart.
Bob's left Jo,
and I don't know what to do
with my hands

or heart or soul.
You count on certain things;
you think they're gold.

To be flayed
and then to be forced
to walk out in the world

among the living
day after day after
day—it's torture.

There is no poultice
for a wound that large.
Time heals, they assure you.

It also abrades,
grates, rends.

You are torn, my friend,
frayed, sucker punched
by life, gutted by love.

Let sunflowers, let lakes,
let islands, let a blossoming son,
let rain, let friends . . .

I, who don't pray,
pray *Let love* . . .

Consolation on the Susitna

I've missed that sound—the quiet *thwt* of my son turning pages.
He's thirteen and has been seduced by the siren song of his cell—
texting and snapchatting relentlessly, suddenly incapable of the
    patience
required for the printed word. He doesn't even realize he doesn't read
    anymore.
But here we are, socked in on the Susitna, Denali nothing more than
    a fog-
shrouded myth. He picks up his mass-market paperback, a Grisham
    thriller, and
sinks in for hours, every couple minutes a whispered *thwt* as
    thumb
and two fingers turn the coarse pulpy paper, the friction from the
    ridges
of his skin catching against the paper's grain just barely audible.
Two straight Alaska-sized disappointments—a silver salmon charter
cancelled and now Denali missing in the mizzle—have dampened
our moods, our once-in-a-lifetime adventure turned ordinary.
But for me now, this almost silent consolation in a small cabin on the
    Susitna:
thwt, thwt, thwt through the drizzly day and into the gray night.

Playing Ping-Pong with My Son

Every time! He beats me every time
now—so different from just last summer.
He revels in destroying me, in
holding me to single digits. While
serving, he admires the new contours
of his shirtless arm. He covers his end
of the table with insouciant glee,
dancing like Cassius Clay, returning one
unreturnable shot after another
while nattering on about movies,
music, friends, and sports. Cursing his
preposterous agility and speed,
I plod like Liston and lunge at air,
about to go down—again. Last week,
the new neighbor swore she'd seen a young
man exiting my house. I denied it
until I realized she meant him:
my teenage son—all sinew, bone, and easy
laughter—making his uncharted way
by burying me a little every day.

Continuity Is for the Birds

They construct their intricate homes each year
without power tools or opposable thumbs.
They raise their young without inoculations,
organized athletics, or college counseling.
Then when the weather becomes unpleasant,
they fly south where the climate is mild
and the days are long. Meanwhile,
we layer up, lean into the bitter wind,
and drink in the dark. And when finally
the dark ages of winter that stretch out
like glacial epochs begin to release their grip,
and mornings arrive on the wings of song,
we rejoice in the return of those small birds
whose departure we had once again failed to mark.

Dogless

The haze hangs low over the stubbled
fields north of County Road 19,
a moody scrim, nearly in-
distinguishable from the darkness.
The day needs a dog: a ram-
bunctious bundle of fur and wiggle
with a relentless tail, an antidote
to December's dictatorship, that
bitter darkness that overtakes us even
before the evening commute begins,
the same darkness which wakes us
in the morning with its dour embrace.
I need some slobber, some jowls,
the sweetly arid scent of paw.

On Pumpkins

They are dumpy orange porpoises diving into a landlocked sea of
    green.
They are the pigs of the fruit world, rooting in a massive mess
of sprawling vines. Acres of these umbilical threads connect them
to the earth, this small home from which none of us wants to be torn.
They squat, make themselves heavy, practice passive resistance.
These oblate and oblong orbs that resist rising mimic the harvest
    moon.
Or is it vice versa? Gravity, not time, is on their side. For all that,
they are jovial, avuncular. They seem to have a sense of humor.
What is the point of a pumpkin? They have no points. Ba-dum-
    bump.
Okay then, what is the purpose of a pumpkin? Like everything else,
they love themselves and want to propagate. They seek posterity
in future generations of pumpkins. And like so much else on earth,
they are sacrificed for our appetites. Their pulp becomes pie.

Pizza and Poetry: A Manifesto
After Frank O'Hara

Because life is terrible, we have pizza
and poems, but rarely do we have them
together. We should. Often.
If we can have paintings about sardines
and poems about oranges, surely
we can have more poems about pizza.

There should be so many more.
About mozzarella and tomato sauce.
About pepperoni and every other topping
that is fine, but not as fine as pepperoni.
About the beauty of the circular form
(both literally and metaphorically).
About the heat and rugged elegance
of the wood-fired oven (often round).
About take-out and delivery and eating it
at home on your couch while
watching tv with someone special.

There should be journals and anthologies
and cookbooks full of pizza poems, towering
piles of them, leaning, and then falling over.

Poems could be printed on take-out boxes
and napkins, so that before dinner you might
read a poem praising pizza, a kind of grace,
then wipe warm grease and sauce from
the corners of your mouth with a poem.
A pragmatic poem! The world
is always in need of pragmatic poems!

In just a few decades America would become
a poetry powerhouse. It would not be uncommon
for us to sweep the medals in the poetry Olympics,
gold, silver, and bronze, round like pizza, like pepperoni,
like the eyes and mouths of my children when I come
home from work on Friday, a hot pizza in my hands.

Clearly the heyday of the pizza poem is still
in front of us. No one has yet been moved to ask:
Where are the great pizza poems of my youth?

Songs in a Narrow Time

I woke up this morning,
eight miles of anxiety
coiled around my neck.

So often we want it to be
a different day than the one it is.

.　　　.　　　.

So often the idea of the thing
is better than the thing itself;

thus maps and books;
thus hope and memory.

.　　　.　　　.

I'm a sucker for a highway,
a gravel road, the siren song of elsewhere,
of nowhere, of in between.

Apparently I want to be somebody else—
at least for a while.

.　　　.　　　.

"You think you can pull that shit in here?" I growl at the dog. "We
have standards," I say, at which point I crack up at the absurdity
of my claim. The dog pulls his poker face tighter. Good boy.
Smart dog.

.　　　.　　　.

I'll be there in a sex,
my son texts.

Autocorrect
incorrect again.

.   .   .

"I was Friday tired on Wednesday," a colleague says.
"Not my can of worms," says another.
"Nothing to ride home about," a student writes.

I feel more tired than I feel like I should feel.
I make plans to write off into the sunset.

.   .   .

The first warm day in May after the snowiest April on record;
I have just come in from doing noble battle with the black
walnuts. The cocky bastards hoisted their little green flags
to the top of their masts before anything else had budded
out, and I dug them up or cut them down when necessary,
their roots corkscrewed deep and strategically close to other
plants, fences, rocks, and sidewalks. In the mirror two dark
lungs of sweat bloom on my chest.

.   .   .

The news anchor intones,
"Apparently this is happening in real time."

.   .   .

They'll send you up the river,
but they'll sell you down the river.

Different rivers, same basic principle.

.   .   .

Days the color of rain,
rain the color of days.

.   .   .

Spring comes late to the north shore,
lilacs and lupine in blossom at the end of June.

Carnivorous butterwort, a hummingbird.

***

Ground Truthing in Hastings, Minnesota

The only skyscraper in Hastings, Minnesota is a bridge.

The Riviera Theater has been renovated—its marquee bold and proud—but screens no movies.

What was William Duffy's farm in Pine Island is 48 miles away. Those two lonely ponies stepped out of the willows 18 miles further south.

John Berryman jumped from the Washington Avenue Bridge nearly 30 miles northwest of here.

The river is muddy, the sky gray.

The leaves have not yet turned, but they are considering it.

A freight train trestles across the river and into town, a common occurrence completely ignored by the locals. I am hypnotized and count the cars in a trance, though I failed to start at the beginning.

Apply Here the sign says, pointing to an empty parking lot.

Of the two kinds of loneliness, this is the good one.

Last time I was here, it was colder and grayer. The wind lived inside my jacket.

Where does contentment go when there's no place to hide?

North Coast

The snow is no surprise here in November.

The north wind is an old friend and rival you have not seen for a while. You've had some hard times over the years, a falling out or two or three. Neither of you is sure what the other will do. You spar, like chess players, like bears.

The waves clamber up the shore, trying to escape the lake.

The cabin shakes like a rusty old biplane that might attempt flight.

The evergreens don their white hats.

Your neighbor fled south weeks ago.

You notice the cattle and horses have gathered by the barn, their strong haunches to the wind, breathing the small clouds that hover in front of their implacable faces and below the dark, heavy clouds that are falling piece by piece to the ground.

You think you could learn something from them and turn your back to the wind. Then it whistles, and you turn back, thinking it might know something you don't.

A Gathering of Stones
After James Richardson and Jeanne Marie Beaumont

It was unclear who among them had called the meeting. Or who would speak first. Concerns had been growing for some time. They tended toward conservatism, fearing change and trusting in silence, which they thought of as a form of prayer, a thing so sacred that it sometimes felt wrong to speak. Plus peer pressure, a societal emphasis on modesty, and perhaps genetics. Over time, they had come to look alike and think alike. Sometimes one would even think it caught a glimpse of itself out of the corner of its eye, but it would turn out to be a different stone, not even related. Though none identified as communist, there was a general egalitarianism, a sense of the greater good that sometimes led to indifference. If no one else was complaining, why should they? But circumstances had changed. It was hard to say precisely how, but everyone, it seemed, was aware of it, somehow felt it. There was a quiet clamoring for something to be done. So they had gathered. Now it was time for one of them to speak, which was no small thing. When one of them said something, it stayed said.

My Nature Poem

My nature poem has air conditioning, but no line breaks. My nature poem doesn't care what your nature poem thinks; that is its nature. Though it has never met a season it didn't like, my nature poem prefers seasons of transition, seclusion, and delusion. There are trees herein, plenty of trees. Ditto for sky and water. It is spacious, capacious. There are very few people, and those who are present are inclined toward silence, except for the children, which like the young of most land species are made of joyful noise and confusion. Not much happens in my nature poem, at least not quickly. My nature poem would like to be wilder—to growl, to rend—but that appears not to be in its nature. It prefers shadows, slinks, burrows, is rarely seen.

The Prose Poem and Common Household Appliances

The prose poem had a healthy respect—admiration even—for common household appliances: the microwave and refrigerator of course, but it was the sturdy washer and dryer—all haunch and torque—that left him speechless. Mesmerized by latitude and longitude, he fantasized about a career as a cartographer. Of football players, he most looked up to offensive linemen. Lace, filigree, and other fancy things were for sonnets and other delicate flowers. All he needed was an open field with space enough to turn around in three times before he slept.

The Prose Poem and the Art Museum

The prose poem had taken to frequenting the art museum, feeling vindicated somehow by the overwhelming number of rectangles and squares, centuries of paintings their makers carefully crafted and framed in his image (or so he liked to think—he knew most of them predated him). A roomful of Rothkos, a few Cornell boxes, a Mondrian, or a shiny Donald Judd piece can bring him to tears. If he ever found the right female prose poem and they made little prose poems together, he would bring them here to this temple built for worshipping the rectilinear shape, this place where he had first felt a pride that made his borders swell.

Notes on the Prose Poem

The prose poem was born from chaos, and unto chaos it will return.

The prose poem refuses the girdle, the suit and tie, jewelry, hats, churches, and courthouses.

The prose poem feels an unrestrained ambivalence about fences but owes a private debt of gratitude to the corn and soybean fields of Iowa.

The prose poem is both particle and wave simultaneously; therefore, it is unconcerned with matters of gender.

There has never been a photo of the prose poem in its natural habitat that isn't inconclusively blurred.

The prose poem is unfit to hold public office.

The prose poem likes to rent a room in unassuming coastal villages, where it spends the night baltering with its first and deepest loves, the moon and sea.

Notes Found on a Napkin in a Diner Outside Akron, Ohio

Let this be the new gospel, murky as the last one, full of contradictions, praise and criticism, and guidelines—impossible guidelines followed only by the saints, who (like the rest of us) fail, but at least they know why they are failing.

Let this be the gospel of the non-believers, for those of that camp need underpinnings as well.

Heretics, it must be said, make life more interesting, bringing light to the darkness and darkness to the light.

Heresy—for some of us—is the source of truth.

Heresy doubts, argues.

Let this be the gospel of blank pages, of the unsaid, the unsayable. Let silence be our song, a hymn to everything we can't understand.

The Years

I have gathered the years in a bunch of plastic garbage bags, which I then tossed in the unused guestroom. Of course, now it is neither unused nor a guestroom; it's where my past is stored, the good moments jumbled up against the bad ones, all tucked away in a room where no one ever goes. Well, I go in there from time to time—say a Friday night when I have no other plans, and I'm feeling lonely. I'll open a bag at random just to see what's in it. There are always some familiar items, and usually a surprise or two, something I had forgotten entirely. The smells are strange and hard to place. Eventually, I get overwhelmed by questions I can't answer. That means it's time to close the bag up, tie the twist tie tight around its neck and toss it in the farthest corner, so the next time I return I will open a different bag. I close the door gently and with a certain solemnity. Some visit to this room—I don't know which one—will be my last. I imagine my sons entering this room after my death, groaning at the mess, wondering what I was thinking holding on to all this junk, saying something about my having been further gone than they realized, and without thinking twice, throwing it all in a rented dumpster. Good boys. Thank you.

Current Events

Here we are in the hottest century humans have ever known, treading the floodwaters of Main Street, navigating between gars and gators, desperate for an espresso martini. Things have not gone quite according to plan, but you can't say we weren't warned, can't say we didn't have fun in our turbo-charged air-conditioned luxury handbaskets. We pledged allegiance to pointless little things and reaped what others sowed. We were never alone, and we never said no. What is the multiverse but a hedge against death? If you're going to drown, you might as well go down live-streaming it, your golden tan glowing in the day's final light.

***

Patriotic

Other than in our glorious national parks,
I rarely feel more patriotic than when driving west,
making my desultory way between the scattered
small towns that are dwindling away, towns
built in part of long silences and failed dreams, and
surrounded by unrelenting space. When I finally step
out of the car, the wind slaps me in the face;
grit that has crossed state lines to greet me
peppers my skin. The leathery-faced locals
show me no warmth, nor should they.
They have put down roots in this stingy sand,
withstood the incessant winds and lack of shade,
put up with the lack of conveniences that would
make a city dweller howl. A church, a run-down
bar, and a dirty gas station; a few ranch houses
and mobile homes, dry thistle-strewn yards
adorned with rusted cars and farm equipment;
the nearest mall, fast food franchise, or big box store
hours away. At such times I find myself despising
the decision-makers of this country—the expensively
coiffed and appareled big shots of Capitol Hill,
Madison Avenue, and Hollywood who have never
seen this road, these fields, this sparsely-populated county.
What do they truly know of this nation? In a neglected
cemetery on the edge of town frequented mostly by deer
and magpies, weeds seared tawny by the sun,
three generations of my family are buried, and so
I pledge allegiance to this dusty whisper of a town,
this place that until I die will never be my own.

Saturday Night, Port Townsend

Flung from the pier, the undersize crab
cartwheels through the air, skinny armored
leg over claw, until it plops back into the
briny bath of the sound. It's a crab's lot—
to scuttle after food in the dark,
to fall for the alluring chicken giblets,
tins of cat food, or fish heads lining
the crabbers' pots, and then to be tossed
back in again. At least until it is large enough
to keep, when such disorienting flights
will suddenly stop. While checking their pots,
the husband and wife from Tacoma
eat take-out pizza in the gathering dark.
The gulls observe no legal limits,
leaving empty overturned shells littering
the wrack line for the morning to discover.

Another Mystery Train

This one is 16 engines long.
That's it. No hoppers, coal cars,
box cars, flat cars, cattle cars,
container cars, tankers, no club car.
Nothing but 16 yellow engines
blazoned with American flags
in far western Wyoming (almost
Idaho), 8 facing north, 8 facing
south. No rock n roll out here.
No Jerry Lee to liberate us
or Elvis to save us. Just
a whole lotta sage going on.
It's the summer of '22,
the end of the empire visible
on the horizon if you're looking
for it. Otherwise, whole lotta
sage going on. I've been driving
down this road 50, 60, 70 years.
Nearly everything alive when
I started is gone now. There's
still plastic, a little neon here
and there, and a train in Western
Wyoming that's 16 engines long.

Letter to Fitz from Big Sky

Dear Greg: How could those trout not go whole hog
for the hoppers you tied me, artificial yellow limbs twitching
desperately in the current, brown and tawny bodies
that would look bewitchingly succulent to me if I were
a gilled thing, a member of the *salmonidae* family, hiding
behind a rock or holding at the end of a riffle, waiting
for just such a moveable feast, perfect replicas of those
leaping *orthoptera* that accompany my every step from car
to river each time I stop? How can they not leap and gulp at
such juicy banquets delivered directly to their kitchen table?
I was afraid they wouldn't let me out of Idaho, Greg. They
were evacuating everyone north of Salmon along 93. Like
a scene from a post-apocalyptic movie, the sky was a solid,
smoke from wildfires so thick I couldn't see across the river,
dusky as late evening in the middle of the day. No sun.
No signs of life but the ghostly sprinklers people left on—
a last desperate attempt to save their homes—and the occasional
grim national guardsmen, menacing in their Hummers
and camouflage. Feeling vaguely criminal for pursuing
pleasure while those who lived there might lose everything and
firefighters flew in from across the country to sleep in tents,
to inhale smoke and heat, to risk their lives, I raced for the border,
fearing at every bend I might be turned back for a three
hundred-mile detour. I made it to Montana, Greg, only
to get skunked day after day in the promised land. Years
of dreaming, months of planning, and now—nothing. Just
last week, catching dappled westslope cutts on the Flathead,
I thought I was ready for the majors, but now I can't
hit my weight. I'm 0 for Southwestern Montana. The Big Hole,
rumored home of the rare and elegant grayling I longed
to see in the wild and brag about catching, was little more
than a trickle through a glade, a lovely place to take a date
for a picnic (I'd encourage you to bring Danielle, but
she'd probably rather be in your driftboat catching fish
or climbing the rock walls around here that are hazy ghosts
at best today), but for fishing? Nah. Nonetheless, like a
five-year old, I dangled an elk hair caddis in a few tiny pools.

I'm glad no one saw that. The Beaverhead and Ruby were running
high and milky green, and anglers along the Madison were lined up
like jets on the O'Hare tarmac. I fished dries and nymphs, terrestrials
and spinners. I fished in sun and shadow. I flailed mightily.
There is no other way to put this, Greg: I failed mightily.
I pushed on through Nevada City, a ghost town where tourists
fluttered about, peering happily in the windows of failed shops.
I drove through Twin Bridges and Ennis, trout towns whose
economies depend on tourists dropping hundreds on rods
and waders and guided trips, unlike cheapskate me asking
for directions and tips, then schmuckishly ducking out empty
handed. Hungry for better water, better luck, a stupid
rookie trout that might fall for my half-assed monkey casting,
I drove on, no plans of stopping here, one of those pricey Western
oases sprung from ski slopes and developers' dreams, but
there was no room at the inn—at any of the many inns—in West
    Yellowstone,
so I dragged my road-weary ass to the car again and raced the
    darkness
to this pleasant overpriced place where the barkeep actually said,
"Yellowstone gets old after a while." I'm toasted, fried, baked.
Too much driving and too much failing. Tomorrow
I'll fish the Gallatin before heading home. Wish me luck.
North Dakota will be twice as long with an empty creel.
                                                —D.

Self Portrait in a Hollywood Western

The whores are looking to separate some lonely men
from their money. The bartender keeps one eye
on the whores and their marks, the other watching
for any untoward business on the barroom floor.
There's a game of cards in the corner, calm for now.
The doors swing open and a stranger enters, a chance
for the sharp to slip an ace up his sleeve. The sad-eyed
young whore who's working a dangerous angle
(revenge? escape?—it isn't clear yet) shoots the barkeep
a look. He nods and feels under the counter for his
gun. Briefly, as the camera pans, so briefly you
probably wouldn't notice him without hitting pause,
there is a nondescript fellow, neither leading man
handsome nor villainously ugly, a little soft
perhaps, not a real wrangler, a mere shadow
in the shadow of the balcony, doing what he's been
told to do, nursing a whiskey. That's me, a coward.
Not a small man nurturing some private grudge and
hoping for glory like Robert Ford or Jack McCall,
just an ordinary everyday coward committed
to saving his own skin, no matter how worthless
it might be. When you hit play, the scene continues.
There are hard-bitten words, unblinking silences.
Before long, some men are separated from their money,
others from their parched lives. When the shooting starts,
I'm the first one on the floor, my table upended
in front of me. Later that night the sad-eyed whore sucks
on her opium pipe, and that extra, the shadow in the
shadow, goes home, and in his notebook by candlelight
on the small table in his small rented room, tries to
piece together everything that has been sundered.

Portrait of My Friend Betty as a Deer Foraging in Her Own Back Yard

If you were a deer, your most reliable
companion would be fear, the radar
antennae of your ears on constant alert,
every noise and movement a potential
threat, everything carrying a brilliant
red warning sign: *Achtung! Danger!*
Suppose your family had lived on this
part of the Pacific Coast for generations
beyond a deer's counting, and suppose
this particular town had grown into
a small city, with all the noise, chaos,
and destruction that entails: forests
buzzsawed into oblivion, earth leveled,
roads paved, and houses constructed.
The cars in the new neighborhood are
bigger and faster than any predator
any deer has ever run from. What,
then, would you do, you with your
lean, graceful limbs, you whose fear
is bigger than your dark eyes and soft
ears? Wouldn't you find your way
to the rambler with the rotting deck
and open gates—a clear invitation—
the one where dandelions and moss
have reclaimed the yard? Wouldn't
such casual disregard make you feel
welcome? Wouldn't you almost forget
your fear and delight in the garden
it seems she planted just for you?

Bus Stop, Lagos
After a photograph by Pieter Hugo

You're waiting for the bus alone
when the devil sits down beside you
on the concrete bench—skin charred,
eyes bloodshot, the four horns
emerging from his scalp sharp
as his dagger-like fingernails—
his thigh pressed up against yours.
You do your best to look impassive,
but he's naked to the waist and massive:
each leg solid as a baobab trunk.
You move your purse downwind,
thank the gods you're wearing
your mother's *gele*, your grandmother's
beaded necklace. You come from royalty,
a family of *obas*, and you always treated
your husband's other wives honorably.
Then last year when your husband—
the last *oba* in the village—died, you
followed your oldest son to this city.
He wears a tie and works in a glass
tower—in the film industry—a kind of magic
you'd never imagined. This new world
is full of strangeness. Riding the bus
to the market, you've never seen
a familiar face—so what's the devil
doing here so far from home?

"The Barn" by John Wilde
Oil on Panel (1954)

The window, the window,
the second story window.
The nude flew out the window.
A pigeon flew from the eaves.
The doll slumped in the wagon.
Perhaps slumped is too strong a word.
What is limper than slumped?
The world was calm in 1954
if you were white and male
and living on a well-groomed farm,
but a nude young woman might crash
through a four-pane window
without wings or hope, screaming
no doubt, and who would hear it
in this pleasant pastoral world?
Only the birds, and they won't say a word.

Today's Image of a Black Hole (The First Ever)

looks like a blurry doughnut,
a ring of fire, an eye in the night,
the shadow of nothing, a navel,
the sun turned inside out, an eclipse,
a zero, someone whistling in the dark,
the business end of a trumpet,
the first appearance of a disappearing act,
the dawn of a new day that has not yet
been named, all my regrets gathered
together, organized, and polished
for public consumption, a lamprey's unforgiving
mouth, the cross-section of a catheter,
a clown with no eyes, a cosmic bagel,
the reinvention of the wheel,
a sink at night, its drain, the sheen
of forever. Or never. An exit of sorts.

The Age of Miracles

I check the traffic on a pocket-sized miracle,
then climb in another miracle and drive to work,
a job I am still grateful to have seventeen years
after they chose the guy with no classroom
experience out of 200 applicants, the guy
who had quit ten jobs in his first ten years
out of college. Between 8:27 and 8:31,
fifteen young living, breathing miracles
enter my room, laughing, joking, a few groaning
about their lack of sleep and the long day ahead,
all oblivious to the miracle of central heating,
which allows us to comfortably discuss one of
Kafka's finer miracles, *The Metamorphosis*, while
outside beautiful white miracles fall from the sky,
and at least for now, not one of us feels like a
cockroach, a miracle of sorts, momentary as it
may be, and none of us is being shot, which
shouldn't be a miracle, but at this time in this
country, it most certainly is, a small miracle
that won't save those who have already been shot
by another citizen exercising his sacred right
to kill another living, breathing miracle.

Troutwatching

No rod, reel, or flies today. For the sake of
family peace, I left the tools of my obsession
at home, but out walking the dog along
shallow, clear Shawneehaw Creek before dinner,
we stop on a wooden footbridge, so I can
watch a little trout holding in the current,
ever attentive for what might come his way
(or even near his way). My patience pays off—
he darts to the surface for an almost
invisible morsel of food, then returns
to the exact same spot, his back blending
in against the mottled bottom of the stream.
I marvel to a passerby that with the quick
current and their tiny brains, they can
distinguish potential food from other
minute detritus drifting past. *It's
their job,* he shrugs. *Good point,* I think—if
they can't figure this out, they won't survive—
the mystery not diminished in the least.
Mesmerized by this young trout (maybe
four inches long) repeating this pattern
(dart and return, dart and return), I stay
until the sky dusks, and I hurry home, late
for dinner, but nourished by what I've seen.

Appalachian Thanksgiving

Blessings on the bufflehead and hellbender.
Blessings on Doe River and Elk Creek.
Blessings on the fog shrouding Blowing Rock.
Blessings on this place absent any flatness.
Blessings on the years of mistakes I've made.
Blessings on my loneliness and hers.
Blessings of her lips and breasts and soft wetness—
blessings for my hands and eyes and tongue.
In gratitude, I pray. Amen. Amen. Amen.

www.ingramcontent.com/pod-product-compliance
Lightning Source LLC
Chambersburg PA
CBHW020222090426
42734CB00008B/1180